Passive Income

20 Stellar Ideas to Win Passive Income

© Copyright 2018 - All rights reserved.

The following eBook is reproduced below with the goal of providing information that is as accurate and reliable as possible. Regardless, purchasing this eBook can be seen as consent to the fact that both the publisher and the author of this book are in no way experts on the topics discussed within and that any recommendations or suggestions that are made herein are for entertainment purposes only. Professionals should be consulted as needed prior to undertaking any of the actions endorsed herein.

This declaration is deemed fair and valid by both the American Bar Association and the Committee of Publishers Association and is legally binding throughout the United States.

Furthermore, the transmission, duplication or reproduction of any of the following work including specific information will be considered an illegal act irrespective of whether it is done electronically or in print. This extends to creating a secondary or tertiary copy of the work or a recorded copy and is only allowed with an express written consent from the publisher. All additional rights are reserved.

The information in the following pages is broadly considered to be a truthful and accurate account of facts and, as such, any inattention, use or misuse of the information in question by the reader will render any resulting actions solely under their purview. There are no scenarios in which the publisher or the original author of this work can be in any fashion deemed liable for any hardship or damages that may befall them after acting on information described herein.

Additionally, the information in the following pages is intended only for informational purposes and should thus be thought of as universal. As befitting its nature, it is presented without assurance regarding its prolonged validity or interim quality. Trademarks that are mentioned are done without written consent and can in no way be considered an endorsement from the trademark holder.

Table of Contents

INTRODUCTION 6

PART I: CREATIVE WAYS TO GENERATE PASSIVE INCOME 10
CHAPTER 1: CREATE BLOGS FOR EARNING A STEADY INCOME 14
CHAPTER 2: MAKE YOUTUBE VIDEOS THAT ATTRACT AN AUDIENCE 18
CHAPTER 3: CREATE REVIEW WEBSITES 24
CHAPTER 4: SELL ONLINE COURSES 29
CHAPTER 5: EARN MONEY THROUGH ONLINE SURVEYS AND PRODUCT SAMPLING 34

PART II: SOME EASY WAYS FOR PROFESSIONALS TO EARN PASSIVE INCOME 38
CHAPTER 6: WRITE A BOOK OR AN EBOOK AND EARN MONEY 41
CHAPTER 7: INVEST YOUR TIME IN DESIGNING GAMES/SOFTWARE/APPS 44
CHAPTER 8: START AN ONLINE STORE WITH DROP SHIPPING 47
CHAPTER 9: EARN MONEY THROUGH PRODUCT DESIGNING 52
CHAPTER 10: EARN MONEY BY SELLING YOUR STOCK PICTURES 55

PART III: WAYS TO EARN PASSIVE INCOME FOR THE SOCIAL MEDIA ENTHUSIASTS 57
CHAPTER 11: SELLING SERVICES ON SOCIAL MEDIA 60

CHAPTER 12: SELLING YOUR PRODUCTS ON
SOCIAL MEDIA 65
CHAPTER 13: SELLING THE PRODUCTS OR
SERVICES OF OTHERS/AFFILIATE
MARKETING 69
CHAPTER 14: EARNING THROUGH
SPONSORSHIPS AND BRAND DEALS 73
CHAPTER 15: EARNING THROUGH
CROWDFUNDING OR DONATIONS FOR YOUR
WORK 77

PART IV: EARN MORE MONEY FROM YOUR
MONEY BY INVESTING *81*
CHAPTER 16: INVEST IN PROPERTY TO MAKE
CAPITAL GAINS 84
CHAPTER 17: RENT A ROOM OR SPACE TO GET
STEADY INCOME 86
CHAPTER 18: PEER-TO-PEER LENDING 88
CHAPTER 19: INVEST IN A BUSINESS AS A
SILENT PARTNER 90
CHAPTER 20: RELY ON DIVIDEND INCOME 92

CONCLUSION *94*

Introduction

Congratulations on downloading this book and thank you for doing so.

This book will discuss how you can create resources and assets that can earn passive income for you. Passive income is an alluring dream, but it can become a reality. If you want to know how, then read on!

Dream of Dreams

Passive income is a tempting and alluring idea. We all dream of assets that can earn money for us while we are not working on them actively. It is a dream come true. Money multiplying while you are vacationing at some exotic place is something everyone aspires to. Yet, in reality, it eludes most of us.

A Reservoir of Perpetual Income

In clear terms, passive income is the fruit of your hard labor done in the past. It is like a perpetual reservoir that keeps filling your wallet. But it isn't free. It doesn't come without effort and enterprise. You can't make money out of thin air. It doesn't come with sheer luck. It is very different from winning a jackpot; a jackpot is a one-time streak. Passive income comes out of substantial work. It isn't a product of luck.

Is It a Reality? Busting the MYTHS

There are a lot of myths surrounding passive income. Some believe that it is not possible for people other than the high and mighty to earn passive income consistently. This is wrong. If you put your efforts in the right direction, then you can build resources for passive income. You need to be focused and determined.

Some people advertise that earning passive income is very easy and you can get filthy rich by investing a fraction of your time. This is simply misleading and incorrect. You will have to put in a lot of effort in the beginning. It requires burning a lot of midnight oil. You will have to sacrifice a great amount of your leisure time at first, but once you have created the asset the amount of work required is minimal and the gains are steady.

Others believe that you need to invest a lot of money and assets to build passive income. This is a half-baked truth. Yes, you will need to build assets, but they don't necessarily have to be money. It is possible to build streams of passive income if you are a creative person, a professional, a social media enthusiast or an investor. You will only need to capitalize on your strengths to build a substantial resource. It is possible for anyone—with or without investing large sums of money.

The Value Proposition

This book will explain some easy ways to take advantage of your strengths to build passive income. It will also discuss in detail the kind of investment required. It will help you to realize the potential inside you.

You Need It and You MUST Get It

Times are tough. The competition is getting fierce. Resources are becoming inadequate, and needs are increasing. It is the need of the hour to supplement income. You have all the right to earn more if you have the potential. This book will help you to explore that potential within you. It will tell you the right ways to put it to use.

This book has divided the ways to earn passive income into four categories based on your potentials and interests. It will not ask you to do something out of this world, but it will compel you to think outside of the box. It will help you to earn steady streams of money while following your passion.

Every effort has been made to ensure it is full of as much useful information as possible, please enjoy!

Part I:
Creative Ways to Generate Passive Income

Get Paid for Your Passions
The internet has given new voice to creative people. Writers, speakers, bloggers, foodies, and fashionists all have a platform to voice their opinions and earn money from it. This presents a unique opportunity for creative and opinionated people. If you also have that spark in you then what's stopping you? There are several ways to get passive income while you follow your dreams and passion.

1. You can earn money by writing blogs
2. You can make money from YouTube videos
3. You can make money providing online courses for people to learn new things
4. You can earn money by taking part in online surveys
5. You can make money creating review websites

Don't Need to Give up Your Day Job

The age of the internet has given you the chance to make your passion a profession. But if you do have a day job and you insist on sticking to it, there's no need to worry. You can unleash your creative genius in your spare time and get paid for it. Isn't this deal sweet? You bet.

The World Is Your Canvas! Get Paid For Your Passions!

This is an information crazy world and the internet has brought it closer. The limitations of distances and boundaries have vanished. People want to experience different cultures, cuisine, tastes, rituals, and traditions, but they might not be willing to leave their homes or even their workstations. The internet has given them the opportunity to experience all these things on the illuminated screen in front of them. The people who help them by taking these experiences to their audiences get paid handsomely. This is the wonderland of the internet.

Shout out and Get Famous

If you have the wanderlust and the power in your words to take your readers with you, then the internet has scores of opportunities for you. If you have the craving to eat and a belly to digest it, then you might as well enjoy the taste too. This would not only foot your bills but make you rich and famous. You don't have to do anything out of the ordinary. Keep following your passion and share your experiences with the world so that the longing souls out there can also enjoy them through your senses. This will get you paid, sometimes much more than your day job. It can create a steady stream of passive income. You might earn while you sleep—literally.

You can do this through all the mediums mentioned above and many more. Create blogs, make videos, do podcasts, write reviews, create online courses, do surveys and make this world a better place.

It's Soul-Satisfying and Money Making

The cherry on the cake is that you will get paid for it. Many YouTubers are earning much more than they did in their previous day jobs. Several bloggers have become celebrities and get treated like one. Podcasters are known across continents, and online courses have given a new lease of life and learning to millions. This is utterly soul-satisfying work, and they are getting paid too. What could be better? They'll keep earning this money for that content for a long time. This is passive income, and it is not very hard to earn.

The next 5 chapters will walk you through how you can earn steady streams of passive income through these modes. Let's Explore!

Chapter 1:

Create Blogs for Earning a Steady Income

Blogs: Evergreen as Before

If you conducted a survey on the ways to earn steadily on the internet, at least fifty percent of respondents would suggest you write a blog. It is such a popular, tried and tested medium. It lets you earn money in more ways than you could imagine. It satisfies your creative urges. It's painless and relieving. But the fact that fascinates me the most is that, apart from all these, it is easily monetizable.

There are several advantages of writing a blog, but let's focus completely on earnings.

There are two main ways a blog earns revenue:

1. Through affiliate marketing
2. Through AdSense

Earnings through Affiliate Marketing

This is the income generated when someone buys a product by clicking a link on your blog. The commission is good. Take, for example, the Grammarly Affiliate Program. You can sign up as an affiliate in Grammarly then write a small blog post about the Grammarly product on your website and place the Grammarly banner anywhere on the page. You'll get paid for promoting the product. Then, when readers sign up using your link, you'll get a commission. The commission is even bigger if they sign up for a premium account.

Earnings through AdSense

Most bloggers employ Google AdSense on their blogs for earning revenue through the ads. The more traffic your blog gets the higher the Google AdSense revenue your blog will generate.

Other Ways a Blog Can Earn Money

These are not the only ways in which you can earn money. If your blog has a good reputation and standing, then people may even ask you to endorse their products or review them. This can also give you some extra money.

Beginning May Be Tedious

However, starting a blog from scratch and bringing traffic to it is cumbersome. But there is a shortcut to that too. Yes, there are shortcuts for most things. You can buy an already running blog.

You Can Buy an Old Blog

Users create thousands of new blogs every day. Some take off instantly, and others are unable to do so well. These blogs get abandoned. But buying them may not be that profitable.

You should look for blogs that are still receiving some traffic. Such blogs can give you a steady stream of passive income. The owners won't put a hefty price on them, and you can get a sweet deal.

If you invest some effort into the content and marketing of these blogs, then they can take off pretty easily. This will increase your monthly revenue prospects.

Start Afresh

If you are thinking of starting a fresh blog, then the first thing to do is focus on a niche. Choose it wisely. All are not equal. Create good content and keep doing that.

New blogs need some time and marketing efforts to take off. But if you are persistent and sincere then there is no reason for them to fail.

There is always a debate about what kind of content sells the best. Some people vouch for evergreen content, and others are in favor of trending topics. To an extent, it is a useless debate. Both have their own pros and cons. The evergreen content requires less effort and management. It is best for those who do not want to put more effort into their blog. The trending topics attract better traffic, but the amount of time required is also high. Choose as best fits your needs and availability.

A Great Source of Passive Income

Blogs are the oldest way of content marketing on the internet and have the highest competition. But they are still very relevant even today. So, if you want to set up a steady source of passive income without investing much, then buying a running blog is the best. If you have things to express and want to earn by voicing your opinions and views, then starting a new blog is the best. Both ways lead to the same end—a steady source of passive income.

Chapter 2:

Make YouTube Videos That Attract an Audience

The world has always had a weakness for visual temptations. We want to get the most through the least efforts. Videos are a combo of both. You get to see instead of reading. This is an easy task and takes less time. We will not diverge into the debate on reading vs. videos, but the important thing is that more people tend to watch videos. They have a bigger and better market. They have greater acceptance in all age groups and all sections of society. This makes videos a favored medium. Google also gives an advantage to videos over written content in its search engine ranking.

YouTube Rules

Multimedia presentation has taken off, and video content is the new trend. YouTube has emerged as the second most used search engine. The number of videos added to YouTube on a daily basis is mind-numbing. The viewership is astonishing, and this opens up new avenues of earning.

If you want to earn money and you have the courage and willingness to face the camera then make YouTube videos.

There are 6 main ways to generate revenue on YouTube:

1. Affiliate Marketing
2. Google AdSense
3. Merchandising
4. Sponsorships
5. Endorsement
6. Product Placement

- **Affiliate Marketing**

You tell your viewers about a product, explain the advantages of using it and encourage them to buy that product. This is the simple concept of affiliate marketing. Once that product is bought using the given link, you get a commission. This is the old and widely practiced method of earning passive income.

- **Google AdSense**

Google gives money to the video makers if the

videos are watched widely. It does so because it runs ads on those videos. The revenue from those ads is shared between the video maker and YouTube. You need to make viral videos to get rich from AdSense money. In fact, some people have got filthy rich doing so.

- **Merchandising**

Once your YouTube channel gets famous, you can sell your merchandise. It is a great way to sell your products. You have your price and your loyal audience.

- **Sponsorships**

Once your videos start getting a good number of views, brands take interest in you. They will sponsor your channel to get their names associated with you. This is a big bucks opportunity. You could earn well and steadily.

- **Endorsement**

This is also an extension of the sponsorship program. Companies want you to endorse their products so that your audience feels a connection with them. This is a great way to earn money. Once your channel has reached a certain amount of subscriber base, you will start getting endorsements. It is also a steady income earned through hard labor.

- **Product Placement**

You can use the products of certain brands in your videos or talk about their advantages in natural form. This is product placement and advertisement. The combination of sponsorship, endorsement, and product placement is very lucrative and desirable. You only need to work on the quality of your videos and improve their content. Once they go viral, the first milestone is achieved.

YouTube has emerged as a giant in showing video content. But it is not alone. There are other sites, too, and they may also pay you for making videos. If you can create viral video content then the opportunities to earn open up.

You Always Need to Remember 4 Important Things:

✓ *Focus on Content*

Content is very important. Some people think that just making viral content is enough. It isn't. You need to make content that's relevant too. You must never compromise on the quality of content.

- *Identify the Viewer Base*

Identify the viewer base of your videos. It is important as you can't serve the same content to all the viewers.

- *Keep Your Content Quality Consistent*

Specific viewer bases watch your videos. When you start rolling out, and your content is of inconsistent quality, or if your content has various irrelevant topics, the viewer base gets confused. There is a lot of competition out there. Keeping the quality of videos consistent is very important.

- *Market Your Content Properly*

To beat the competition, you will have to market your content aggressively. Use content marketing, social media marketing, and other mediums for attracting viewers.

This medium can fetch you steady passive income for a long time. The focus should always be on creating good quality content and remaining consistent. It may be a hobby for you, but it is also a job for you that will earn money. You must never take overly long breaks. This may reflect your inconsistency. The subscribers may start looking elsewhere. Building an asset requires hard work and diligence. You need to work on it. Once you have done your part, you can relax and enjoy the money.

Chapter 3:

Create Review Websites

Reviews: Solving the Problem

The economists say that problem of choice is the biggest problem in this world. When we have to make a choice, we prefer to take the road often traveled. I guess that's why Robert Frost had such a dilemma about traveling on "The road not taken." Jokes apart, choosing things is difficult at times. We try not to make mistakes. That's why we like to hear the opinions of the people who have used them. Whether it is a book, movie, food joint or a nightclub, we want to know the experience people had there before we go. This is a safe approach and a wise one too.

But someone has to take the plunge and use it for the first time. What if you make it your business to do that? It is fun, adventurous and will help you in earning passive income.

Reviews are Important

User reviews are very important these days. When Google starts giving importance to something, consider it to be important. You will be doing a great service by doing reviews of all these things. But this isn't just social service, you will be earning from it too.

Imagine you started reading a 300-page novel and somehow completed it with great remorse as it was not up to the mark. Why should we all go through the same experience? In another case, a book is really good, but people are not reading it because it comes from a fairly new author. That would be bad. Your honest reviews can help in spreading the good word. The question then arises, how are you going to monetize it? The answer is simple, through affiliate marketing and AdSense. Believe me, it isn't going to make you a millionaire, but if your passion is reading, you'll get tons of free books and traffic to your website. This means money, and it is good.

Review websites come in many forms. Before setting up a review website, it is important that you clearly identify your niche.

Once you are through with that, you must ask yourself 4 important questions:

1. What do you want to review?
2. Is there a specific subcategory in your review category?
3. Do you have a marketing strategy?
4. How will you earn?

Let's discuss these questions in detail.

What do you want to review?

The choice is important as it determines the kind of traffic you will get. You can review all sorts of things like books, movies, hotels, products or anything else. The choice is completely yours. It must be your comfort zone. You will have to do it for a long time and consistently.

Is there a specific subcategory in your review category?

'A rose by any name' might have worked for Shakespeare, but it wouldn't work for you. You will have to identify your target audience. You can't expect readers of romance to come to you for science fiction or thriller reviews. This becomes all the more important when you go for technical books as they have a small but impressive readership. But that would need expertise in the field. Only venture into it if you possess that. Identifying the niche correctly solves the confusion. It sets the goals and achievement objectives clearly in front of you.

Do you have a marketing strategy?

Review websites are a dime a dozen. Most of them are buried in oblivion waiting for their obituaries to be written, but no one seems to find time for that. You don't want that. You want to earn money. It will only come if you have visitors on your site, which will not happen on its own. You will have to form a strategy. If you are thinking of going for any specialized field then finding the target audience is easy. They are small in number and easily identifiable. You can use blog postings, articles, and other marketing content to attract readership. Using email marketing is also a good way to build a loyal readership.

How will you earn?

The best way to earn commission is, again, by affiliate marketing. You can do that by giving a book an honest review, and the people who like the sound of the book may purchase it *using your link*. Doing movie reviews is a good way to earn Google AdSense money. The audience base is large. It wants to know what they are about to experience. The same is true of reviewing other things. Each has a potential. You just need to find a voice. Express yourself honestly and sincerely. The visitors must not feel cheated or misled. They will come flocking to your blog.

Chapter 4:

Sell Online Courses

Do you love teaching people? Do you think you have some skill that others don't possess? Do you wish to teach those skills to others?

If you answered yes, then you can do all this. This is the most soul-satisfying work in the world. This is the purest form of happiness. But the awesomeness doesn't stop here. You can also earn money and fame from it.

Selling online courses is one of the best ways to earn passive income. It is passive in real terms as you wouldn't be doing any work in real time but you'd still be earning money. You only prepare the online courses once and get passive income from them as long as they are in demand.

All you need is the knowledge of something that is in demand—a craft, a skill, a language, coding, application development or anything else. You must have a knack for making people understand it easily and simply. Online courses have opened up new avenues for those who have something to teach and even for those who want to learn. They are simple, easy and affordable. There are no complicated procedures for enrollment or headache of managing big or small classes. Any number of students can learn together or at times of their choice. It offers complete freedom for everyone, and these courses are as effective as real classes only more efficient. Here, the student comes with a desire to learn and not out of compulsion to get a degree or due to peer pressure.

How Do You Make Money?

It offers a great opportunity to earn money. How much you would earn would depend on the type of course and platform you choose. If the course you are offering is in good demand, then the sky is the limit for your earnings. Lynda, Shaw Academy, Khan Academy, Udemy are some of the popular platforms that offer such courses. You can start your own, put up a membership or course fee and enjoy.

Things to Remember

- *It is not as easy as it sounds*

Knowing how to teach and having a passion for it is not enough. You will have to do the groundwork before you begin. A lot of time, some money and an insane amount of time will be needed in the beginning. The hardest part will be to choose a course that is in demand yet few people are offering it. You must find such a course for which people are ready to pay money.

- *You will have to put in a lot of hard work*

Preparing an online course is at least 5 times more work than writing an eBook. There is a lot of coursework, assignments, practice material, and promotional content to be prepared for it. It will take a lot of your time.

- *Promotion is important*

You will have to publicize your course on the internet. It takes patience and hard work. Until people know about it, they are not going to take an interest in it. Your marketing strategy must be sorted.

There Are 2 Most Popular Mediums for Earning Money

❖ Open your own members-only multimedia-driven website

This is a great way to earn. You will have complete control over the money you earn. Create a full-fledged multimedia website and put a membership fee on the courses. Market your courses properly and enjoy the money that flows in. The only drawback with this way is that you may not have very great traffic or a wider reach. Still, you can get people through affiliate marketing and email marketing. Marketing aggressively is the keyword here. Make people realize the potential of the course. The better you present and the more value you give the higher the chance of getting the returns.

❖ YouTube Videos

This is another way of earning money. However, you will have to depend on the money earned from Google AdSense. You can't put a price on the videos as YouTube videos are generally free. But you will have a wider reach and greater audience. If you want money with greater satisfaction of doing good for the public, then this is the medium for you. You can also have a mixed approach. Give insights into the course on YouTube and sell the full course through your own membership-based website. The key here is in building a clientele. If the content is good, then you will get customers through referrals and word of mouth publicity too.

Whatever medium you choose, selling an online course is a great way to earn passive income. In addition to that, it gives the great joy of sharing knowledge.

Chapter 5:

Earn Money through Online Surveys and Product Sampling

This is ideal work for those who have time to spare. Suppose you spend too much time in front of the television. You like giving feedback and have opinions about things. You like to test new things. Then this could be the ideal opportunity for you to earn passive income.

Online surveys and product sampling opportunities are available in large numbers. I wouldn't say they pay ludicrous amounts of money, yet you could get paid for answering a few simple questions based on your experience. All this while you continue enjoying your favorite show. If you sign up for product sampling programs, you can get free samples in exchange for your reviews.

Make Money in Your Leisure Time

The best thing about this work is that it doesn't require any specific skill or enterprise. Anyone can do it. It is easy, and you can do it in your free time. It is easy money. Over time you will get experienced and start getting better paid and have ample opportunities.

Get Free Products to Try

Consumer research companies are always looking for people who are willing to try new products. Your reviews help the product in improving quality and getting a response from the buyers. They will give you the products for free.

As I mentioned, in the beginning, these aren't big buck opportunities. But these aren't difficult jobs either. You can do them anywhere anytime.

Here Are Some Simple Tips to Do Better in the Game:

Do's

- You must set up a new dedicated email for taking online surveys. You don't want your original inbox to get cluttered or miss any opportunities.
- If you have more free time then why not sign up for more than one survey site? You'll never run out of surveys.
- Keep updating your profile at regular

intervals. This helps you in getting shortlisted for better surveys.
- Keep a check on the privacy settings and the money you are earning from specific sites. It will show your earning capabilities.

Don'ts

- Never register on sites that ask for a membership fee. These aren't legit.
- Never reveal confidential information about yourself like your credit card details, social security number, etc.
- Always remain cautious of malware and spams. Most of the survey sites may have these issues.
- This cannot be the main source of earning a livelihood. It will always remain a supplemental source.

Product Sampling

Product Sampling or consumer surveying is different from an online survey. Here the companies want you to try their product. They can't offer you any fee for this. That way you may not give honest reviews in the temptation of more income. Yet, you can get free products to try. All you would need to do is write reviews and talk about your experiences. This is not direct income, but think of the money you might have to spend in buying those products. Money saved is money earned.

These methods will help you in earning while you are literally using your time for doing something else. It is a passive income. The earnings won't be high, but this is not your full-time job either.

Part II:

Some Easy Ways for Professionals to Earn Passive Income

If you are a professional, then you already know what hard work is. You have toiled hard and made your way up. You have tasted success through work, and you know that it will always bear sweet fruits. Why not put in some extra efforts to keep earning while you relax? Think of it as a bonus income. If luck favors then, who knows, this income may well surpass the income from your full-time work.

Build an Asset

For professionals, there are many ways to earn passive income. You can extend your current work as overtime to get extra money, but that's overtaxing yourself. Besides, it wouldn't give you repeated returns. Passive income means that you create an asset and then earn money from it over a long period. An asset doesn't necessarily mean money or property. Intellectual property is also an asset. You can write, design games or applications, write a program, build successful websites and earn money. If you have some interest and you are good at it then why not make use of it professionally? Selling stock pictures is also one way of earning consistent results.

In This Part We Will Explore 5 Ways to Earn Money by Making Use of Your Professional Skills:

- Write a blog and earn a royalty
- Invest your time in designing games/software/apps
- Start an online store with drop shipping
- Earn money through product designing
- Earn money by selling your stock pictures

Earn Money by Sharing Your Skill

You don't have to do something out of the ordinary to earn extra money. You just have to share your knowledge and experience with everyone, and they will pay to enjoy it. It can be in the form of a book, program, website, design or anything else. If you have something to showcase then the world is waiting to see it.

Get a Steady Stream of Passive Income

All you need is the will and willingness to execute your plan. In the beginning, it will involve some extra work. You might want to relax after a long day and may have to sacrifice it. But the fruit will be sweeter in the form of long-lasting returns. Some people keep getting royalties years after their book was published. An app can be worth millions. A design can make you rich and famous. You only need to make up your mind and have a plan.

Enrich People and Get Rich

There will be competition, hardships and times when things are going south. But don't worry. Being a professional you know it is a part of life. Follow it persistently, and you will make your mark. You need to share your knowledge and skill honestly with people. Tell them the stories you have, the knowledge you treasure and the information you possess. Allow them to experience all of this through your applications, and they'll come in droves.

Does this sound exciting to you? The next 5 chapters will explain the various ways to make use of your professional experience to earn passive income. It will explain the hardships to come and the milestones to be achieved. Whatever the result may be, you are bound to have a memorable journey.

Chapter 6:

Write a Book or an eBook and Earn Money

Let the World Know What You Have Learned

Do you like telling stories? Do you know something from which others can benefit? Can you teach the world something useful? Do you love writing? If your answer was affirmative to any of these questions, then there are promising opportunities waiting for you.

Books have long been the best friend of mankind, so we have been told, and as a professional who knows this better? You have gained a lot by spending on books. Now it's your turn to reap the benefits.

You can write books on your area of expertise and get money from their sales or even royalty money if it works really well. You can choose a high-demand niche and write books on it. Either way, it is money, and it is good.

There are several ways you can earn money writing books. You can either write books for publications and earn royalties or you can write eBooks and sell them on Amazon or other marketplaces and affiliate websites.

Some of the Best Ways to Earn through Writing Are:

- Write Books

Books are an eternal source of knowledge. People treasure them, and writers earn through them. You can also have a piece of this pie. You can approach various publications with book ideas, and if they get approved, you can earn money upfront. The goodness doesn't end here. You can keep getting royalties for years to come. This is a truly passive income.

- Sell eBooks in the Marketplace

Writing eBooks is comparatively easy. You can trim the content in parts and make several eBooks. Selling eBooks at marketplaces is quite easy. Most of the job is done by the marketplaces, and you can run ads and do a bit of marketing for generating sales. Keep the price competitive, and you can get good sales. If you have a stellar idea but think that you might not have the perfect skills to pen an eBook, then you can also outsource it. The book would still be yours, and you can reap its benefits.

- Sell Them through Affiliate Websites

Selling eBooks through affiliate links is also a good idea. The marketing is done by the affiliate websites for a commission, and a major portion of the sales come to you. This way you can get a good amount of passive income.

- Write eBooks for Kindle and iBooks

If you already have an eBook, you can repackage it and sell it at a slightly higher price exclusively for Kindle or iBooks. This way you'll make more money with the same effort.

This is a good mode of earning passive income for a longer period. You would be sharing your knowledge and earning from it. So, if you want to make some more money from your knowledge and experience, don't yet throw in the towel; instead, sit down to write a book.

Chapter 7:

Invest Your Time in Designing Games/Software/Apps

Build Something Exciting

Computers and the internet have changed the world as we know it today. New technologies have sprung up, and they have opened the door to opportunity. People want better user experience on the internet. They want easier ways to do things. New and interesting games excite them. They want better applications to make things easier for them. New avenues of opportunities have opened up. Do you have what it takes to make things interesting for users? If your answer is a yes then there are possibilities of passive income for you.

Coding Can Take You Places

This is an exciting opportunity for people with knowledge of coding. Software development and game and application designing are trending. You can make a lot of money through them. If you have knowledge of these then most probably you are working in an IT firm. But are you content with the fact that most of the money earned from your hard work is taken by your company? Of course, it invests in you and the overhead. But your knowledge is still with you. Thousands of professionals are making use of this knowledge to earn money by working for some extra time when they have it to spare. You can design games, applications and software programs. You can collaborate or outsource the extra work and prepare a program that earns money for you. It is easy money for you and brings immense satisfaction. Watching your creation win hearts and kudos is very satisfying.

Catch the Train Even If You Don't Know Coding

Your investment is pretty low as you know how to code. You have the network to do the testing, designing, and other jobs. So it'd take up less time and resources. But if you are new to the circuit and still want to jump in, you can. You can outsource everything and get the final product. The investment would be comparatively high and the risks greater. The success of a game or application depends on the service it provides and the quality it holds. You will have to take your chances.

Find the Right Marketplace

You can put a price on your application, game or software and sell it online through various websites and marketplaces. You can also sell the licenses to get long-term income. The play stores are very crowded in general. They have hundreds of thousands of applications, yet new and useful applications can make their space.

The Apple store is a much better market for selling your applications.

You might as well create a derivative app for an existing app. Provide the things people are looking for, and you can hit gold.

Software/app/game development isn't very passive as you'd need to provide support and updates. But it is still good money for a long time. You shouldn't miss the chance.

Chapter 8:

Start an Online Store with Drop Shipping

Entrepreneurship is not for everyone. One needs to have the enterprise, persistence, and risk-taking abilities. Yet, people with such abilities get stuck at odd jobs. They make loads of money for others while getting a small piece of it themselves. Yet, they can't get out because they need money to survive. This creates discomfort. If you picture yourself in the same spot then creating a drop shipping store might be a solution for you.

You can start your own online store with minimum investment and risk. You only need to have a sharp eye to find the right product and management skills. You can begin this in your spare time and keep getting passive income for a long time. Drop shipping is a great idea for enterprising individuals.

Find a Niche

The biggest challenge in starting a drop shipping store is finding the right niche. There are big sharks in the market like Amazon, eBay and hundreds of others. They have millions of products, worldwide reach, and a smooth, well-oiled delivery system. Yet, you can survive if you find the right niche—a niche that has low competition but a good number of buyers; an area that needs special attention, detail or customization, which others can't provide but you can.

Conduct Thorough Research on the Target Keywords

This is the first step to success. You must invest your time and expertise in finding the right keywords searched by the users. They must have proportionate demand. If you find one, you can move ahead.

Window Shop at Marketplaces

Visit the popular marketplaces. See if they are selling those products or not. If yes then explore the look, quality, and pricing. This will give you an idea for whether you can survive the competition or not.

Find the Best Social Media Platform for Your Niche

If something has a demand, the social media platforms are sure to make a buzz about it. This is very natural. Find the discussions. Get a grip on the trends and the talk. Understand if it has juice for you or not. Platforms like Reddit, Facebook and YouTube will tell you the scope if you look closely enough.

Pick a Niche

Now finally decide the niche you want to pick. Be wise and choose prudently. There is no point of return beyond this point. You will have to commit from this point ahead. There will be a real investment, however small.

Find Suppliers and Contact the Best Fit

Look for the suppliers of those products. Filter them as per your need and establish contact. You will have to share information, company details and tax information with them. Think of a name and business strategy.

Create a Brand

Now create a brand. You will go public now. Your brand must reflect the product and your idea of it. It must be well thought out. It should be striking, catchy and easy to remember.

Start Telling Your Story

Form a brand story. This is important to establish contact with the users and build a connection. It must have an appeal. This gives it a personal touch and better grip.

Create a Website

Build a website. In today's world, this shouldn't be tough. You can do it yourself or outsource it. But pay attention to the marketing and e-commerce aspect of the website. It shouldn't be fussy, slow or confusing.

Set Products and Pricing

Now set all the products you want to sell and the prices they'll have. Remember you are not a lone wolf in the market. There are beasts of prey, the predators, and sharks. You must be different, competitive and better in some respect.

Launch Your Website

You are set to sail. Launch your website. Test it thoroughly. Find all the problems before the customers face them. You have set up a complete business.

Go All out on Marketing

Go full throttle. No holds barred when it comes to marketing your websites and products. Take professional help in marketing. The initial phase is the most challenging. Building trust is the toughest. Once you are rolling in the market things get easier. But you will have to take the first step to reach this point.

Give Yourself a Chance

If you do this correctly, then you are likely to be on the path to success. Life is short and full of ambitions but covered with excuses. Give yourself a chance. A chance that you rightly deserve. If you fail, there will be no regret that you could have achieved it. If you succeed, you'll reach your rightful place.

Chapter 9:

Earn Money through Product Designing

Make Things Better

There's nothing in this world that can't be made better. One man understood this fact, and he created Apple, the world's most trusted and loved brand. The gift of designing and the ability to see things differently is precious. If you have it, don't waste it. It can make a lot of money for you.

Earn from Your Designing Talent

Product designing is a sphere with a lot of interest. People want to buy new, innovatively designed products. Demand is at a new high. This forms a great opportunity for people with skill. Designing is a gift that is inherent. If you have it in you then why not make use of it?

Design Anything You Like

You can design mugs, T-shirts, eyewear, home decor items, and the list is endless. Every niche has a need for this skill. You will be in demand. The bonus point is that you'll be doing what you love. The money is good, and the appreciation is better.

There are plenty of websites like Zazzle, Redbubble, Teespring, Etsy, and CafePress that will buy your designs. You can choose your niche and sail free. This is a great way to earn passive income in addition to your regular work. If you have a good hand and a spirit to excel, you can even earn more than your day job pays.

You can even sell the pictures clicked by you to these websites for printing. They can also fetch you money.

Capitalize on Your Potential

The crux is that you must think differently. You can choose any art form. The type of designs you create can also vary. They must have appeal. Make funny designs or designs with emotional appeal. Anything and everything can have buyers. With time, patience and practice you'll get a grip on the pulse of the market. From this point onwards things will start to look up.

So, don't waste your time and talent. Explore your potential and put it to use so that you can earn more from it. Capitalizing on potential is the only way of being superbly efficient. Things that have been termed as worthless hobbies aren't the same in this age of the internet. They have gained value. There is a need to explore it and bring it to the frontlines. Every talent can earn passive income for you.

Chapter 10:

Earn Money by Selling Your Stock Pictures

Among the most popular fads these days are traveling and photography. Armed with high power cameras, individuals like to click pictures of anything and everything. It costs virtually nothing. Ask the poor souls of the camera film era that bled for every picture. However, this new convenience is not only good for flaunting captivating shots with your friends and peers, you can even earn from it. Selling stock photos on photography websites like Shutterstock or Getty images will fetch you money. You can earn money from your hobby.

There Are 2 Revenue Models

1. Flat Fee

The stock websites can give you a flat fee for your photos. This is a one-time opportunity. You sell the pictures to them along with the copyright to use them. This isn't bad because you have hundreds and thousands more photos. It can become a good source of passive income.

2. Percentage

You can also get a percentage of the profit from the sale of your photographs every time they are bought. This is a great form of residual income. The photo can last a very long time on such portals and keep bringing in money for you.

How to Do It

The process is very simple. You have to make an account on these websites and create your portfolio. Properly tagging the pictures with descriptions is a better way to generate higher sales. The users will be able to find them easily.

You can make accounts on several stock photo websites to earn more from these pictures. Remember this is a true passive income. Once you upload the pictures, there is no follow-up required. As and when they get sold, you earn.

Part III:

Ways to Earn Passive Income for the Social Media Enthusiasts

Social media is the flavor of the season. It is a virtual world that has gained new dimensions in the current age. You spend most of your leisure time on social media, interacting with people and building connections. Your friend lists have hundreds and thousands of names, people you personally know and some you have only met online. Your following is great and you influence a lot of people in many ways. You are witty and a lot of people like the jokes you crack online. If you have any of these qualities or the potential to acquire them, then you have the potential to become an influencer. Social media can become a potential source of passive income for you. This part is exclusively for you. Read VERY carefully.

From an Eyesore to Eye Candy

Social media has taken a lot of flak from the intellectual world and the sociologists. But it is and will remain an apple of the eyes of the marketers. Social media is a platform where people connect with each other personally. They get influenced by people they meet and like to follow them and listen to them. This opens a new opportunity for marketers. They are more than willing to connect with such individuals who have a strong friends list and a good following. They want their products and content to have a great reach. They want people whom others trust and follow. So, if you have a great presence on social media, then there is an opportunity for you. Your hours spent on social media and the hard work are about to pay you and pay you CONTINUOUSLY and well.

No Need to Go an Extra Mile

The better aspect of this is that it is easier than it sounds. You only need to keep doing what you are doing. You will not have to go out of the line. Marketers want exposure for their products or content. You will have to share or post their content on your network, and you will get paid for that. This is a great opportunity. An interest that took up most of your time has matured enough to give you returns. If you are new to the social media circuit, then you can start building the network as it can work in the same way for you. It is an opportunity open to everyone.

Learn the Ways to Earn Passive Income through Social Media

This part will discuss how you can earn money through your social media activities. It is legit, easy and highly rewarding. You won't have to push any product down the throat of your contacts. You won't have to market aggressively. Keep doing what you are doing. You will only have to post content of the marketers, share it and like it. This will give them exposure, and you will get money for it. A steady stream of money for the leisure work you have done.

If this excites you, then the next 5 chapters are just for you. Understand how you can earn money from social media.

Chapter 11:

Selling Services on Social Media

If you are reading this book it means that you have aspirations and ambition. It means you are enterprising. This is a good sign and an advantage to start with.

If you can offer any kind of service, then social media platforms can give you the necessary exposure. In monetary terms, it is marketing money. You can leverage the power of social media to market the services offered by you. The people in your network or the ones following you are likely to trust you for that service and purchase it whenever required. This is a great advantage offered by social media, and, until this point, I haven't even started talking about marketing the services of others. We'll come to it slowly.

Social media is a great place to sell your services. The followers know your style and personality and are familiar with the kind of user experience you will provide. This creates a very fertile ground for you. You can advertise any skill or trade you practice or an interest you cherish, and you can earn money for that.

Facebook provides great exposure as the users are interconnected and the reach is wide. Instagram has a wide scope for showcasing talent as people follow personalities closely. If your service has substance, then it can make many eyeballs move. Be it physical fitness, diet, fashion, or any other craft, the social media platform has takers for all. You can leverage the power of your social media platform to influence others and sell your services to the world.

Yet, the most effective marketing method in the world is still word of mouth publicity. This is just like that; a reference coming from a referral. You can get the price you want if you can convey the message properly and also reach a wide audience. This kind of exposure is invaluable, and it is coming for free. You will not have to spend a dime on it. Strengthen your social media presence and make yourself relevant and authoritative on the subject. This will give you a great advantage over the competition.

3 Steps to Earning Money by Selling Services on Social Media

1. Carve Out Your Personality on Social Media

You must represent the service you want to sell. This is the primary step. People won't just believe what you're saying. Your personality must speak for itself.

2. Establish Yourself as an Authority

It is important that you exhibit command over the subject. Having authority on the subject will not only attract followers, it will also lure advertisers. This is very important for making it a value proposition.

3. Consistently Follow It

It is very important that, once you have got the value, you keep following it regularly. Even a small amount of effort on a regular basis will ensure that your passive income never dries up. You will keep building a new fan base and increase your authority.

2 Very Important Things to Remember

1. Be Authentic
2. Provide Value

ALWAYS Be Authentic

Social media reputation is very fragile. It is highly influenced by user reviews and opinions. If you are advertising any kind of service, then you must remember that you are vouching for it. The people influenced by you may try those services if needed. The service must reflect your persona. It should be a part of your online personality. This will make you more trustworthy in your followers' eyes. Surveys have revealed that 71% of the top influencers feel that honesty is a very important trait in the field. You must represent in your image what you are selling to others. This way the content will become relevant and appealing.

You MUST Provide Value

This is the hard but very important part. Fame goes to the heads of some people with a good following on social media platforms like Twitter, Instagram, and Facebook. They think they can sell anything forever. It is a grave mistake. Over a period of time, their campaigns will start losing power, and they'll lose money. Simply doing sponsored postings on Instagram or Twitter is not enough. You need to add value to it. Back it up with reviews, posts, and blogs so that the followers can have confidence in the product and you. This is a more sustainable way to earn income.

Selling services is a great way to earn money, and it is quite easy on the social media platforms. So, if you offer any kind of service or have an interest in a specific field, you can market it and earn passive income.

Chapter 12:

Selling Your Products on Social Media

Social media presents a great opportunity for people who want to sell their products online. Some experts say that social media is not the right platform to sell things, but this is an academic point to debate. It is a platform where you are amidst like-minded people, those people who are interacting with you and have a connection with you. Some admire you, others follow, and many will be highly influenced. If you have a product, then what better market can you get? Marketing your product to these people is easy, effortless and free.

This is an investment free opportunity whereas any other medium of publicity may require bags full of money to begin with. Those mediums offer no guarantee of results and ROI (Return on Investment) of such advertisements is usually low. We all have grown up watching tasteless TV commercials, front page ads, and humongous billboards but also know that they cost a fortune. For a budding business, this is the best mode of advertisement. It has such a great potential that it has even made established brands and businesses kneel to its power. You can earn by selling the products of others too. This is the easiest way to earn money through social media.

But—and there always is a BUT—the roads to fame, power and money are never that easy. You will have to work your way to it. If you want to become a successful marketer on social media and earn money from it, then you will have to move methodically. You will have to establish yourself as an authority and influencer in that category.

For ease of understanding, let's take the example of online games. They are a craze, and millions of people play and discuss them aggressively. If you want to sell or promote games, then you will have to establish yourself in that category. The question pops up, how do you do it?

Build Genuine Interest in It

This is the first step towards gaining authority on any subject, whether it is games, books, a hobby or any other product. You must understand the product inside out. Your familiarity must be above the superficial level. People won't follow you if you do not have anything deeper to offer them.

Give, Give and Give

This is an extension of the earlier point, but it goes beyond just the interest level. You must be able to offer insights into the interests or the product. You must remain consistent in your approach towards giving new information. This will help in establishing you as an authority on the subject and over a period of time people will pay heed.

Explore New Things

As an expert, people's expectations of you will be high. They will expect more information and insights. You must explore more and divulge further. This will help in increasing your fan base and following. At this stage, you will start getting noticed. People will value your opinions and suggestions. This is the stage where brands get interested in you.

Never Stop Exploring and Giving

Once you have achieved a good standing in the category, it is important that you keep pursuing it. You will have brands coming after you and money will follow. But it is very important that you keep exploring new things and never cease to surprise your following with new information.

This will be easy work for you but worth every minute of your time.

The product can be anything, but your interest in it must be genuine. Always remember that one can fool some people some of the time, but no one can fool everyone all the time. Stopping and getting stagnant will hurt your passive income badly at this stage.

This is a great way to earn passive income through social media as you will just be pursuing your hobby or passion and subsequently earning from it.

You will always have a steady stream of money pouring in from your marketing endeavors. It is an opportunity you must grab if you want to make every minute of your time spent on social media worthwhile.

Chapter 13:

Selling the Products or Services of Others/Affiliate Marketing

This is a direct opportunity to earn money through social media platforms. You will have to promote products and services offered by others. It is an easy job if you have a great presence on the platforms. But it will also need your time and efforts in promoting the products.

You can earn money by selling the products or services of others through various means. Good content and persistent efforts will play an important part here. Some people do it as a full-time job, and it pays well. So, if you have any apprehensions about the opportunities to earn, you must shun them.

Get Better Reach

The first and foremost need for this game is a good following. The money lies in the number of products sold, downloads, shares or traffic achieved. It is a conversion in any form. To get higher conversion, your reach must be wide. To earn well, you must expand your base farther.

Form a Strategy and Sign up for Affiliate Programs

Clickbank, CJ Affiliate, and Amazon offer some of the most popular affiliate programs. Signing up is easy, but the strategy to earn money should be well thought out in advance. If you try to push products and links down the throat of your network, then you may end up losing it. Very aggressive marketing may give away your plan. You can't keep posting pictures of the products on your Instagram, Twitter or Facebook wall. This will make people avoid you, and there will be no business. Always give out more than you seek. Add value to your posts. Post honest reviews of the product. Give out impressive content that makes people realize the value of the product. Add a personal touch to the posts so that people can connect better.

Keep Building Your Base

Always remember a basic thing: any company or brand will only approach you if you have a good following. The affiliate programs will only work if people click on the links posted by you. Otherwise, the whole program will become a dud.

You must always keep expanding your base. The most reliable way of doing this is by adding value to your post. This may sound like preaching, but believe me; this is the most reliable way of doing it. Remember on the social media platforms you are not the only one doing it. Even the platforms are also doing it. The users want trust before anything. Pushy tactics do not work anymore but value does. You must add value.

Do Not Overkill

Overdoing things has its drawbacks. It can make you stand out as aggressive, predatory and untrustworthy. There are high chances that you might get into the scanner of the social media platform algorithms. After all, they are meant for socializing and not selling. Yet, if you place the links strategically and cloak them well then there is no better medium than social media platforms. Use shortened URLs, cloak them and use them wisely in the posts. Spreading them everywhere might prove to be counterproductive.

Remember:

- Don't shoot yourself in the foot

You must realize that you cannot use social media platforms as your personal public address system for product promotion. This is a great put off and eats up your following. No one wants junk in their posts. The internet is enough for that. There is already too much trash flying around on the internet so try not to add to it. If you start promoting random things for the sake of earning money, then your chances of earning even a dime will dwindle. You must not forget the basic rule of social media marketing, and that is building authority. You must choose the products to promote wisely. There are hundreds of products to promote on Clickbank and other affiliate sites. Pick a product belonging to your area of expertise and interest and then build your campaign.

- Do not rush

In the beginning, it may look tiring, hard and worthless and, on many occasions, it may well turn out to be so. But persistence and hard work always pay off. Once you have built a campaign, there is no looking back from there.

If you want to give it a try, then you can build a stream of passive income from it.

Chapter 14:

Earning through Sponsorships and Brand Deals

This is a point where earnings get big, but the going gets easy. Yet, reaching this point is the toughest part of the ordeal. Getting sponsorships and brand deals is a hard nut to crack. There are several parameters used by companies for choosing the best marketer. It is important that you qualify on all or most of them.

The Ideal Conditions for Getting Brand Deals Are:

- ✓ You must have a great follower or subscriber base

This is a primary condition for any brand to come to you for promoting their content. After all, better reach, coverage, and viewership is their main motto. They want their product and brand to get noticed, liked, talked about and bought. So, if you have a big follower base or have subscribers ranging in the thousands, then you have all the probability of getting shortlisted for brand deals and sponsorships.

This is a tough task. The follower base is usually volatile, and you have to put in some really hard work to retain it. But it is a doable task and people are doing it. If you have decided to get there, then you must take as a word of caution that you should always develop a specialty or area of expertise because companies like to target specific customer bases. A person engaging the audience of their interest is a good candidate for offering brand deals. But, take my word for it, once you reach that point, things get awesome.

- ✓ You must be a force to reckon with

It goes without saying that companies are looking for value for their money. They want to invest money where they get the best returns. Influencers in specific fields are a good candidate in this area. If you are someone who has great grip on the subject and people follow what you say in the field, then companies are bound to be interested in you. This will only be possible if you have selected a niche domain and work consistently upon it. It is an important criterion.

Your Content Must be Going Viral Frequently

As Bill Gates once said, content is the king on the internet, its place is paramount. The internet is driven by the exchange of knowledge. Even if you are promoting a product, its reach, substance, and following are very important. Superficial content doesn't last long on the internet and gets lost in oblivion. It is very important that you pay great attention to the quality of your content. It is sad that sometimes even great content fails to make its mark on the internet, but the chances of worthless content going viral are impossibly low. For a brand to approach you, it is very important that you create great content—content that is awesome, jaw-dropping, awe-inspiring or shocking and leaves people wondering and longing for more. If you have that ability, then the brands may take you even if you have a low fan base.

This is a very challenging job but not an impossible one. Aim for it, and you'll make great content at least.

- ✓ You are providing immense value

As mentioned earlier, the brands are looking for someone who can add value. A boring and spineless campaign that looks mechanical is worthless to anyone. The brands know that they are already doing a better job than that and won't get any better returns from it. They are looking for value that you can add to it through strategically promoting the content. If you are up for it, then there are very high chances that you will become the blue-eyed boy of the social media marketing scene.

There is a saying that there is no free lunch in this world. Yet, if you sow well, you can reap better. If you have worked hard on your social media circuit and planned your moves, then there will be no looking back for you. The crux is to become meaningful and relevant to the work you are doing. If you are really doing such work, then you might hold more value for the brands than certain celebrities who are giving no real value to the brand. I'd again like to reiterate the fact that it is a tough task, but it is very much possible.

Chapter 15:

Earning through Crowdfunding or Donations for Your Work

Crowdfunding: A Ray of Hope for Artists

Crowdfunding sites have come as a breath of fresh air for artists and creative people. If you have a way with any musical instrument, singing, dancing or you are a magician with a brush then you are in luck. Crowdfunding websites like Patreon have shown a new ray of hope to artists.

Get Paid for Performing the Artform You Love

Suppose you are a singer, dancer, painter or a cartoonist and want to improve your art but don't have money. You can ask people to support you by donating money. This is a great way to keep the spirit of art alive.

Give and Take Relationship

Websites like Patreon and Kickstart fund those people who are taking up new projects or following their passion. It is a two-way street. You are sharing your art or project with the public, and, in return, they are donating money to you. This is a very novel concept, and it has really taken off.

Sustainable Income through Shared Load

You can make YouTube videos, record songs, upload sketches or paintings and ask the admirers of your art form to donate. The donations come from separate people, hence no single individual has to bear all the load. It is easy and very convenient. You can make your profile on the crowdfunding sites and get a link to share.

Promote Your Link through Social Media

If you have a good social media presence and people in your circuit like what you do, then you can promote your Patreon page in your network. Remember that the more people sign up for your crowdfunding the better income you'll have. You don't need to spend any money, you don't have to ask for money from people, only prepare and upload great content. If your content is likable, then you will get good money for it.

Can Anyone Get Money from Patreon or Other Crowdfunding Sites?

If you think there is less competition out there, then you are disillusioned and living in a wonderland. The competition is tough and getting projects on the altar difficult. You will have to show real potential for getting selected and follow strict guidelines. Once your project is approved for crowdfunding, you will have to keep some things in mind to keep getting passive income.

Important Things to Remember

- ✓ *Always Set Achievable Goals for Your Projects*

On these sites, people are donating to keep you motivated. But motivation must not start out looking like greed. You must set realistic goals for yourself so that they are met easily. This will help you in understanding your potential as well as keep the stream of funds flowing. You must state the reasons for funds clearly so that people understand the urgency and need. If you need money for gear, instruments, training, survival, make it clear to your patrons. This will state your honesty and people will donate accordingly.

- ✓ *Showcase Your Work Consistently*

This is of great importance. You want to get something from people, and therefore you must give with greater zeal. People posting once in a while soon lose their patrons and they aren't considered serious. If you are an artist, you must have the urgency to showcase your art to the world. Keep the flame alive to engage your patrons.

- ✓ *Give Back to Your Patrons*

People are donating to you for your art. They might not expect anything from you in return. But pampering them with rewards like free lessons, tips, exclusive content, etc. wouldn't hurt anyone. This keeps them motivated, and they will feel a personal connection with you. It also gives you referrals and more patrons.

Social media platforms will help you in finding these patrons and taking your art to them. Once they reach you donating might be easy, but you are a gem to be discovered yet. You will have to shout out your art to them on the social media platforms. Make full use of the potential of these sites and give new wings to your artistic aspirations.

Part IV:

Earn More Money From Your Money by Investing

Money begets money. It is a very old and proven saying. The wealthy have more ways to keep getting wealthier. The poor find few ladders. If you have wealth, why not put it to use to earn more money? You do it all the time. The money in your bank account is earning interest. You are practically doing nothing to increase the interest. The only problem is that the bank's interest is peanuts.

You can earn much more from your money if you invest in a bit wisely. There may be some initial work, but, in the end, the money will be bringing in more wealth.

Investing Small

There are numerous ways in which your wealth can earn more, but, for the sake of convenience, we'll only discuss the ways in which you can gain even by investing modest amounts. Whether you have a lot to invest or small savings, everything works almost in the same way. The returns remain somewhat proportionate to your investment.

Some of the Best Ways to Earn Money by Investing Are:

- Invest in property to make capital gains
- Rent a room or empty space to earn money
- Peer-to-peer lending
- Invest in a business as a silent partner
- Rely on dividend income

Start Modestly, Play Safe

The amount of money you can invest in all these ways varies. Nowadays, there are several options to invest in property even if you do not have greater savings. Crowdfunding property is also a good option if you do not have much money to invest. The returns are great. In the same way, you can also do peer-to-peer lending through lending platforms. The minimum required sum is low, and the returns are much better than the bank. Making use of your extra room or empty space for renting is a fine way of earning rental income.

Make the Most of It from Your Savings

Your aim should always be to invest safely. The greater the projected returns the higher the risk. Whenever you get a proposal for earning a filthy amount of money, you must remember this. Yet, slow and steady wins the race won't work very much for you in today's fast-paced world.

The midway is to choose investment options that offer safe yet higher returns. The risk should be low, and the returns must be satisfactory.

If the idea works for you, then the next 5 chapters are just for you.

Chapter 16:

Invest in Property to Make Capital Gains

This is probably the safest mode of investment. The chances of property appreciation are always there. The rent money is always sweet. It isn't laced with the sweat of your brow. It is steady. You are always in control. It may require some management of the property, but that's easy work, and you can even outsource it to property managers. The biggest incentive is in the form of capital gain at the time of sale. This amount can be much higher than the interest acquired from the money in the banks.

Choose the Property Wisely

The real trick is investing in the right property. Various factors contribute to the value appreciation of the property. Things like the location and future projects in the area are some of them. Taking them into consideration is very important.

The best way to do this is to buy a property that has a high probability of getting rented. This way a portion of your mortgage repayment will come from the rent. You will be able to pay off the loan easily. By the time you need to sell it the property will be paid off. It will have gained value.

Invest in REITs

If you do not have the kind of money to invest in real estate but want to start then you can also invest in Real Estate Investment Trusts (REITs). You can start with very small amounts of money. REITs are managed by professionals and run on crowdfunding. Small investors put in their money, and the trusts purchase properties. They manage those properties and promise great returns.

Start Early

The important thing is to start somewhere. If you keep thinking of saving so much one day that you can buy a property upfront then either you are daydreaming or you are doing something great. If not, then start early. As you start getting returns on your small investment, you will develop an interest in investing more.

Investment in property is a great source of passive income. Technology has opened doors for small investors too. If you also want to get a piece of it then start now.

Chapter 17:

Rent a Room or Space to Get Steady Income

Rent with Air B&B

Renting is a good idea. A tried and tested one for decades and centuries. It is no secret. But things have been happening quite fast in the past few years. Companies like Air B&B have made renting space to travelers easy and profitable. You can rent your rooms or empty space and earn money from it. The best thing is that the prices are really good. It works well for both the parties, you and the traveler. It is a win-win situation.

Utilize Your Spare Space

How often your property gets rented and the price it gets would depend upon various factors. Things like the city, tourist influx, and type of accommodation offered would matter a lot. You can also rent out the empty space of your garage, too, for parking. Everything has a value. Why not utilize it for earning some money?

It's Not That Passive, but It Still is Money

If you really want to make passive income, then this idea may not be very striking for you as a lot of effort is required from your side too. But it is an idea that works and gives money.

If you have a property that you can rent out, you can get a steady income from it and there will be minor management required. You can lay low pretty easily. So, look at your options and the effort you are ready to put in. This will help you in deciding what works best for you.

Chapter 18:

Peer-to-Peer Lending

Become a Money Lender

This idea is fascinating. We have all been getting peanuts from the banks in the name of interest. When we ask for loans, they demand exorbitant rates. What if you could get those rates on your money? Then you think you don't have that kind of money. The fun part is you don't even need it. You could use even a modest sum for peer-to-peer lending and earn handsome interest.

How Does This Work?

It is centered on the idea of convenience. People need small loans from time to time. The banks are reluctant in disbursing loans quickly without much paperwork and conditions. There are lending clubs that can do this for you efficiently. You can start with very small amounts. Diversify your risk by giving small portions of your investment to a large number of people. This lowers your risk in case any loan turns bad. In that case, too, you'll have very little to lose.

Low Risk

The returns are obviously higher than the ones offered by the banks. There is some amount of risk involved, but you can mitigate it by investing in a number of loans.

A Good Way to Save Money

This is not a very high return or exciting passive income idea, but it will surely give you returns. Your money will get invested, and you can use it as a saving.

If you are wondering how to invest your money, then this can be a good idea for small lenders. There is very little work for you to do as the management is done by the clubs. This is a way to earn passive income.

Chapter 19:

Invest in a Business as a Silent Partner

This is a heavy idea I admit. Investing in a business about which you don't know anything can be risky. But think of it as an investment opportunity. You actually don't have to run the business or take part in its day-to-day activities. You are just acquiring an equity position in the business. Once you invest, you will have a share in the profit and loss of the business.

Invest in a Locally Established Business

For beginners, investing in a well-to-do local business that needs money for expansion is the best idea. It is a favorable situation for both parties. You can get great returns on your money without doing much as you will be a silent partner. The business owner will be getting the interest free money for the business.

Calculate the Risk to Reward Ratio

There are some risks as it goes with any investment. The business can go bad. But that would be a test of your prudence. You can't make an investment without looking at the position of the business in the market. It is important that you do your research properly.

Consider all the available options. See the standing of the business in the market. Look at the future prospects. Discuss in detail the profit sharing model. Know about the owner distribution schedule. It is always wise to have a periodical distribution of profit. Investing in a sale out basis is a risky condition.

A Small Investment Can Give Passive Income

The venture capitalists or the angel investors also do the same. They just take higher risks, invest more money and gain better profits. You are starting low. But this is a real passive income. You don't have to take part in the business activities. No headache of the business is yours. You will just invest and cash out from time to time. You can explore this option for getting steady passive income.

Chapter 20:

Rely on Dividend Income

Investing in high yield dividend stocks has always been a lucrative idea. These pay you better money than interest, and you keep getting passive income from them. There is some risk as market forces act upon them. Still, they pay you well.

There Are 2 Types of Income You Can Get

- Dividend
- Capital Gains

Dividends

Dividends come at regular intervals. They will be a source of passive income. You won't have to do much in managing them. The companies in which you have invested are already doing their work.

Capital Gains

There is every likelihood that the stocks in which you have invested appreciate. You are investing in a long-term perspective, and it happens. In that case, you will also earn capital gains. It can be huge at times. But keep your hopes modest.

Investing in stocks is easy these days. You can open an account with any brokerage firm and get assistance in building a portfolio. Before opening an account with any brokerage firm do your research properly. Brokerage firms charge a fee for their services, and it would be good if you were familiar with the costs.

Conclusion

Thank you for making it through to the end of this book, let's hope it was informative and able to provide you with all of the tools you need to achieve your goals whatever they may be.

This book has covered 20 passive income ideas that can help you in supplementing your income. Some ideas may work better for you and others may not. It is at your discretion what to choose or leave. What's important is initiative. The world is moving at a very fast pace. It is getting costlier by the day. Needs are increasing, and earnings are stagnant. A little extra income without doing anything wrong, illegal or out of line is always worth a shot.

The book has explored the ideas based on specific talents hidden in you and the expertise possessed. These ideas do not require high investment, great involvement or risk-taking. They are simple tasks to be done with diligence and sincerity. It a waste to leave your talent unexplored and underutilized. When you have it, why not benefit from it?

These ideas can help you not only in opening up sources for passive income but also in helping you to push yourself a bit harder. Over a period of time, we all get complacent and relaxed. This is not going to help anyone. Your efforts can help you and others.

These are simple, initiative driven ideas involving simple tasks. You can outsource the parts you feel are complicated. You can sublet jobs. The idea is to create a stream of extra income from some work done in your spare time.

You can build good income sources depending on the kind of work you do and knowledge you possess. If you have been searching for new ideas to earn more money at a steady level, then this book is for you.

Finally, if you found this book useful in any way, a review on Amazon is always appreciated!

www.ingramcontent.com/pod-product-compliance
Lightning Source LLC
Chambersburg PA
CBHW031448210526
45464CB00005B/2371